TRINITY
COLLEGE LONDON PRESS

GRADE

04

BASS

Published by
Trinity College London Press Ltd
trinitycollege.com

Registered in England
Company no. 09726123

Photography by Zute Lightfoot, lightfootphoto.com

© Copyright 2017 Trinity College London Press Ltd
Third impression, November 2020

Printed in England by Caligraving Ltd

Parental and Teacher Guidance:

The songs in Trinity's Rock & Pop syllabus have been arranged
to represent the artists' original recordings as closely and
authentically as possible. Popular music frequently deals with
subject matter that some may find offensive or challenging.
It is possible that the songs may include material that some
might find unsuitable for use with younger learners.

We recommend that parents and teachers exercise their own
judgement to satisfy themselves that the lyrics of selected
songs are appropriate for the students concerned. As you
will be aware, there is no requirement that all songs in this
syllabus must be learned. Trinity does not associate itself with,
adopt or endorse any of the opinions or views expressed in
the selected songs.

THE EXAM AT A GLANCE

In your exam you will perform a set of three songs and one of the session skills assessments. You can choose the order of your set list.

SONG 1

Choose a song from this book.

SONG 2

Choose *either* a different song from this book
or a song from the list of additional Trinity Rock & Pop arrangements, available at trinityrock.com
or a song you have chosen yourself: this could be your own cover version or a song that you have written. It should be at the same level as the songs in this book and match the parameters at trinityrock.com

SONG 3: TECHNICAL FOCUS

Song 3 is designed to help you develop specific and relevant techniques in performance. Choose one of the technical focus songs from this book, which cover two specific technical elements.

SESSION SKILLS

Choose *either* **playback** *or* **improvising**.

Session skills are an essential part of every Rock & Pop exam. They are designed to help you develop the techniques music industry performers need.

Sample tests are available in our *Session Skills* books and free examples can be downloaded from trinityrock.com

ACCESS ALL AREAS

GET THE FULL ROCK & POP EXPERIENCE ONLINE AT TRINITYROCK.COM

We have created a range of digital resources to support your learning and give you insider information from the music industry, available online. You will find support, advice and digital content on:

- Songs, performance and technique
- Session skills
- The music industry

You can access tips and tricks from industry professionals featuring:

- Bite-sized videos that include tips from professional musicians on techniques used in the songs
- 'Producer's notes' on the tracks, to increase your knowledge of rock and pop
- Blog posts on performance tips, musical styles, developing technique and advice from the music industry

JOIN US ONLINE AT:

 /TRINITYROCKANDPOP    @TRINITY_ROCK    /TRINITYROCKANDPOP   and at **TRINITYROCK.COM**

CONTENTS

THE AUDIO

Professional demo & backing tracks can be downloaded free, see inside cover for details.

Music preparation and book layout by Andrew Skirrow for Camden Music Services
Music consultants: Nick Crispin, Chris Walters, Christopher Hussey, Mike Mansbridge
Drums recorded by Cab Grant and Jake Watson at AllStar Studios, Chelmsford
All other audio arranged, recorded & produced by Tom Fleming
Bass arrangements by Sam Burgess & Ben Heartland

Musicians
Bass: Sam Burgess
Drums: George Double
Guitar: Tom Fleming
Vocals: Bo Walton, Alison Symons, Brendan Reilly, Tom Adamson, Hayley Sanderson

YOUR
PAGE
NOTES

TECHNICAL FOCUS

FOREVER

HAIM

WORDS AND MUSIC: ALANA HAIM, DANIELLE HAIM, ESTE HAIM

SINGLE BY
Haim

ALBUM
Days Are Gone

B-SIDE
**Better Off
Go Slow
Forever
(Dan Lissvik Remix)**

RELEASED
12 October 2012

RECORDED
2012

LABEL
Polydor

WRITERS
**Alana Haim
Danielle Haim
Este Haim**

PRODUCERS
**Ludwig Göransson
Haim
Ariel Rechtshaid**

Singer-songwriting sisters Este (bass), Danielle (guitar, drums) and Alana Haim (guitar, keyboard) were born and raised in California's San Fernando Valley and formed Haim in 2007. Dash Hutton, son of Three Dog Night singer Danny Hutton, joined on drums in 2012.

'Forever' was Haim's introductory calling card, released as the title track of an EP that was initially available as a free download from the band's website in early 2012. *NME* singled out 'Forever' as one of its '50 Best Tracks of 2012', labelling it 'four minutes of pop brilliance that sounds at once fresh but classic, painstakingly constructed but viscerally exciting.' The band's breezy combination of 70s soft rock and modern-day R&B brought them international recognition as well as high-profile tour support slots with Mumford & Sons, Taylor Swift and Florence and the Machine. Their 2013 album *Days Are Gone*, which featured 'Forever', reached No. 6 in the US and debuted at No. 1 in the UK.

TECHNICAL FOCUS

Two technical focus elements are featured in this song:

- Note lengths
- Repeated semiquavers with crescendo

You'll need to take great care of your **note lengths** in this song. The bass mainly plays short detached notes, which should be performed with a consistent style and attack, ensuring that all rests are observed. In the breakdown, the **repeated semiquavers with crescendo** will need to be rhythmic, with the crescendo evenly distributed over the three and a half bars' duration.

5

TECHNICAL FOCUS
FOREVER

ALANA HAIM, DANIELLE HAIM, ESTE HAIM

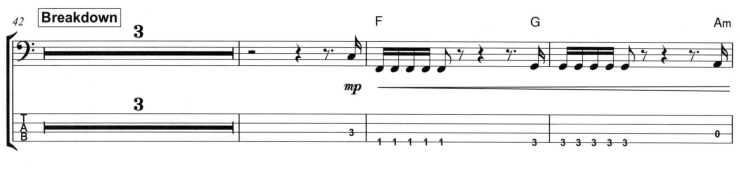

I NEVER LOVED A MAN (THE WAY I LOVE YOU)
ARETHA FRANKLIN

WORDS AND MUSIC: RONNIE SHANNON

SINGLE BY
Aretha Franklin

ALBUM
I Never Loved a Man the Way I Love You

B-SIDE
Do Right Woman, Do Right Man

RELEASED
10 March 1967 (album)

RECORDED
24 January 1967

LABEL
Atlantic

WRITER
Ronnie Shannon

PRODUCER
Jerry Wexler

Born in Memphis, Tennessee in 1942, Aretha Franklin grew up singing gospel in her father's church before signing her first record deal at the age of 18. The first female performer to be inducted into the Rock and Roll Hall of Fame, a 2010 poll by *Rolling Stone* magazine placed her at No. 1 in the 100 Greatest Singers of All Time.

Aretha Franklin recorded nine albums for Columbia Records between 1960 and 1966. Jerry Wexler signed her to Atlantic Records in 1967 and arranged for her to record with an all-white group of Southern session musicians called the Muscle Shoals Rhythm Section, who had played on Percy Sledge's 'When a Man Loves a Woman' and Wilson Pickett's 'Mustang Sally'. Written specifically for Franklin by songwriter Ronnie Shannon, 'I Never Loved a Man (The Way I Love You)' was released as Franklin's debut single with the label and it became her first top-ten hit (as well as topping the US R&B chart for seven weeks). It also provided Franklin with the title of her tenth album, widely regarded as an all-time classic album and one that established the singer as 'The Queen of Soul'.

⚡ PERFORMANCE TIPS

This song is unusual for its $\frac{3}{4}$ time swing rhythm, which is its main challenge. The rhythm in bars 3 and 4 should underpin what you play for the rest of the song, so you may want to practise just these bars until you have captured the laid-back feel. The triplets, which first appear in bar 6, are really just a decoration of bars 3-4, even when they become more complex at bar 14 and elsewhere. Look out for the tricky pattern at bars 19-20, and spread the crescendos evenly over the bars where these are marked.

I NEVER LOVED A MAN (THE WAY I LOVE YOU)

WORDS AND MUSIC: RONNIE SHANNON

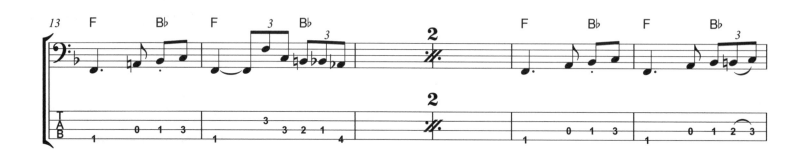

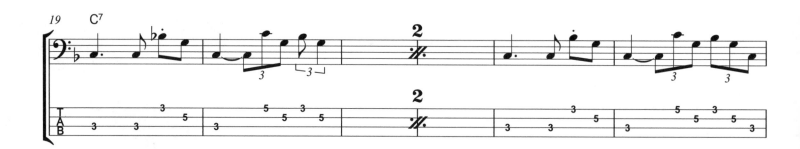

YOUR
PAGE
NOTES

I WISH
STEVIE WONDER

WORDS AND MUSIC: STEVIE WONDER

SINGLE BY
Stevie Wonder

ALBUM
Songs in the Key of Life

B-SIDE
You and I

RELEASED
**28 September 1976
(album)
November 1976
(single)**

RECORDED
**1974-1976
Crystal Sound, Hollywood
California, USA
Record Plant, Los Angeles
California, USA
Record Plant, Sausalito
California, USA
The Hit Factory, New
York City, New York, USA
(album)**

LABEL
Tamla

WRITER
Stevie Wonder

PRODUCER
Stevie Wonder

Stevie Wonder is one of the most remarkable figures in popular music. A child prodigy who has been blind since birth, he mastered piano, harmonica and drums by the age of ten before being signed by Motown boss Berry Gordy aged 11. Two years later he scored his first US No. 1 single, the first of many hits, and went on to write, perform and produce a number of classic albums.

'I Wish' was the first single to be released from Wonder's 1976 self-produced double album *Songs in the Key of Life*, a commercial and critical hit and the third album in Billboard chart history to debut at No. 1. Wonder came up with 'I Wish' after attending a Motown company picnic in the summer of 76, an afternoon involving games that reminded him of his childhood, he said:

> I had such a good time at the picnic that I went to Crystal Recording Studio right afterward and the vibe came right to my mind.

The song was Wonder's fifth No. 1 in America and earned him a Grammy Award for Best Male R&B Vocal Performance. The bouncy, infectious bassline was played by Nathan Watts, who played with Wonder for the first time on the album and has done so on almost all subsequent albums, as well as serving as his musical director.

⚡ PERFORMANCE TIPS

Listen to the original version of this song to get a sense of how to articulate the quavers, which should have a feeling of energy and bounce. Bars 25-28 are an opportunity to be stylish – you can afford to draw attention to the bass here, observing the articulation to capture the effect of the original.

I WISH

WORDS AND MUSIC: STEVIE WONDER

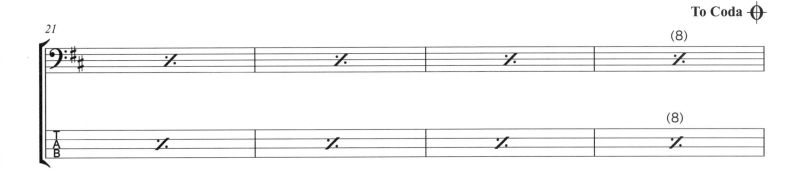

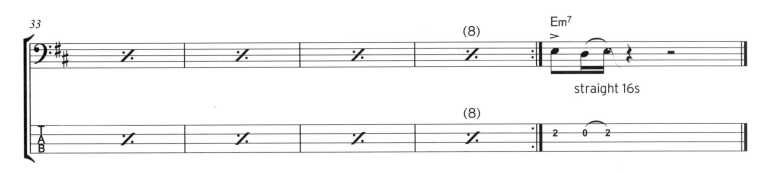

YOUR
PAGE
NOTES

TECHNICAL FOCUS

RIFF
RAFF
AC/DC

WORDS AND MUSIC: ANGUS YOUNG, MALCOLM YOUNG, BON SCOTT

SINGLE BY
AC/DC

ALBUM
Powerage

RELEASED
5 May 1978

RECORDED
**January–March 1978
Albert Studios
Sydney, Australia**

LABEL
Atlantic

WRITERS
**Angus Young
Malcolm Young
Bon Scott**

PRODUCERS
**Harry Vanda
George Young**

One of the world's best-selling rock bands, AC/DC were formed in Sydney, Australia, by guitarist brothers Malcolm and Angus Young. Bon Scott was the band's original singer until his death in 1980, after which Brian Johnson became frontman. The band's long-term rhythm section has comprised of Cliff Williams on bass and Phil Rudd on drums.

Probably AC/DC's most breakneck-paced rocker, 'Riff Raff' is a track from the band's fifth album, 1978's *Powerage* (the first to feature bassist Cliff Williams, who would remain with the band until 2016). Although at the time it was the band's least successful album internationally, it remains the first choice among AC/DC aficionados and musicians of assorted generations – Keith Richards, Gene Simmons of Kiss and Eddie Van Halen have all named it as their favourite, as has Justin Hawkins of The Darkness, who stated: 'For me, when it comes to AC/DC, you cannot better *Powerage*.' *Ultimate Classic Rock* said of 'Riff Raff':

> This pedal-to-the-metal hard rocker finds both Malcolm and Angus peeling off deft fingerings in between cathartic power chords with abandon. AC/DC defined.

TECHNICAL FOCUS

Two technical focus elements are featured in this song:

- Syncopation
- Stamina

The opening riff of this song is a challenge of **syncopation**. Count this rhythm carefully until you can feel it securely, and note how it becomes embedded in the repeated quavers of the verse. The whole song is a test of **stamina**, requiring you to maintain consistent articulation and a strong rhythmic feel.

RIFF RAFF

WORDS AND MUSIC:
ANGUS YOUNG, MALCOLM YOUNG, BON SCOTT

Intro

Heavy Rock ♩ = 182 (1½ bars count-in)

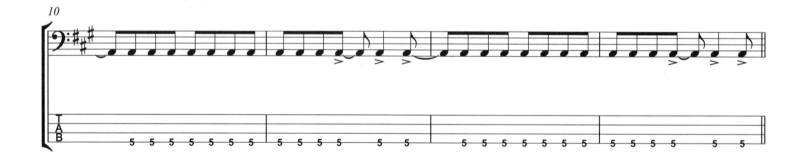

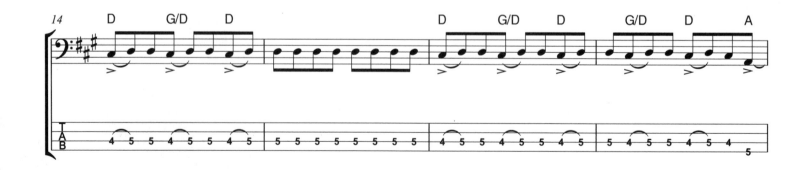

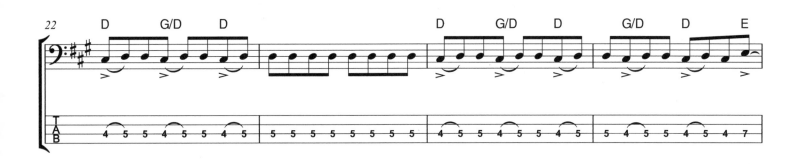

Verse

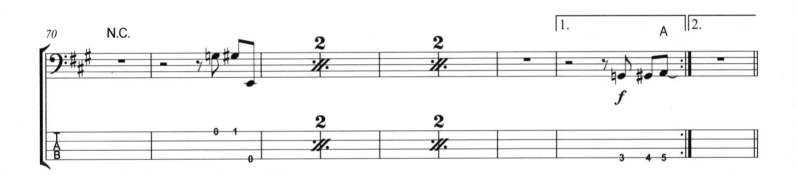

SINGLE BY
Ocean Colour Scene

ALBUM
Moseley Shoals

RELEASED
5 February 1996

LABEL
Island

WRITERS
Simon Fowler
Steve Cradock
Oscar Harrison
Damon Minchella

PRODUCER
Brendan Lynch

THE RIVERBOAT SONG
OCEAN COLOUR SCENE

WORDS AND MUSIC: SIMON FOWLER, STEVE CRADOCK
OSCAR HARRISON, DAMON MINCHELLA

Formed in Moseley, Birmingham in 1989, English rock band Ocean Colour Scene attained success at the height of the 90s Britpop era. They comprised Simon Fowler (vocals, acoustic guitar), Steve Cradock (guitar, piano), Damon Minchella (bass) and Oscar Harrison (drums).

Featuring Paul Weller on organ, 'The Riverboat Song', the lead single from Ocean Colour Scene's second album, 1996's *Moseley Shoals*, was the band's debut UK top-20 hit. It was championed by BBC Radio 1 DJ Chris Evans, who played it frequently on his breakfast show as well as using the opening instrumental section as the theme for his TV programme *TFI Friday*. It was released the same week that *TFI Friday* debuted, and the band performed the song live as the show's first musical guests. *Moseley Shoals* was released two months later and rose to No. 2 on four separate occasions and for a total of seven weeks between April and September 1996, kept off the top for six of those weeks by Alanis Morissette's *Jagged Little Pill*.

⚡ PERFORMANCE TIPS

The bass part of this song, which is often in unison with the guitar, requires rhythmic precision and stamina. The time signature is unusual, and while the bass pattern feels like two group of three crotchets per bar, there is sometimes tension with the drums, which can sound like three groups of two crotchets. This means you'll need a strong internal sense of the pulse. There is a variety of articulation to observe throughout, particularly in the chorus.

THE RIVERBOAT SONG

WORDS AND MUSIC:
SIMON FOWLER, STEVE CRADOCK
OSCAR HARRISON, DAMON MINCHELLA

Intro

Rock, slightly swung ♩ = 215 (2 bars count-in)

(guitar)

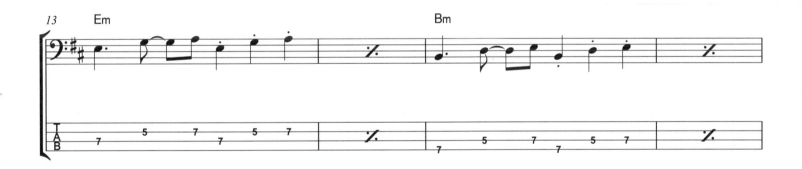

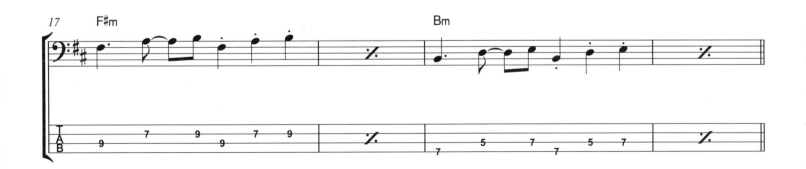

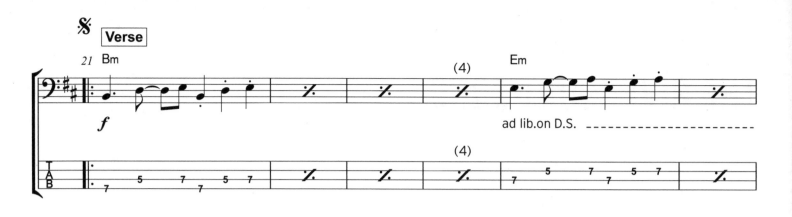

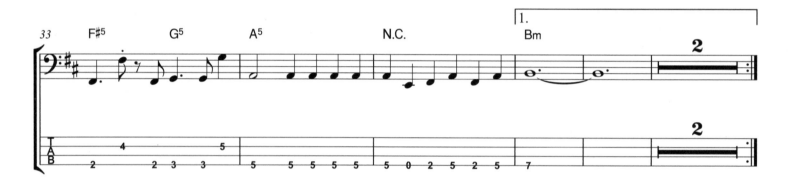

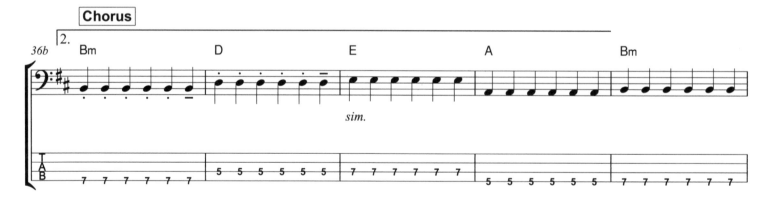

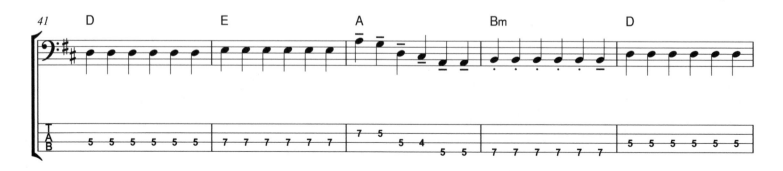

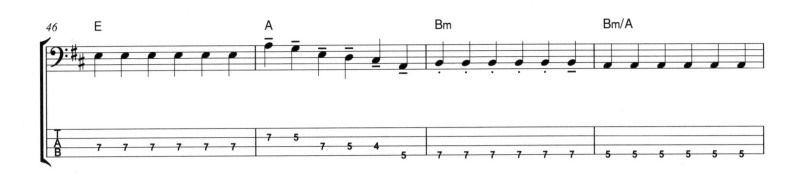

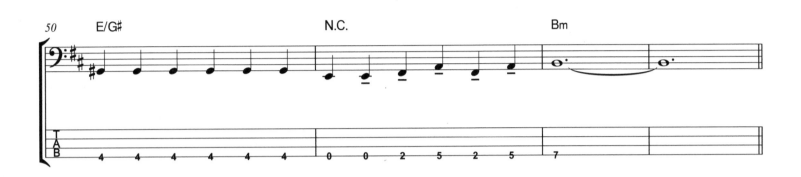

Guitar solo

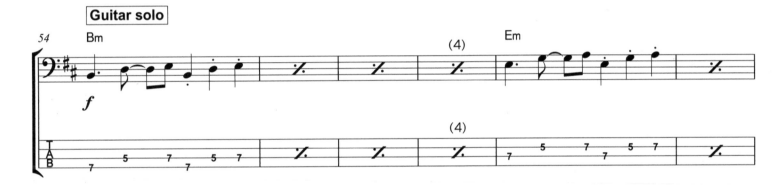

D.S. al Coda

Coda

YOUR
PAGE
NOTES

TECHNICAL FOCUS

SLEDGE-HAMMER

PETER GABRIEL

WORDS AND MUSIC: PETER GABRIEL

SINGLE BY
Peter Gabriel

ALBUM
So

B-SIDE
Don't Break this Rhythm

RELEASED
25 April 1986

RECORDED
1985
Ashcombe House, Bath
Somerset, England

LABEL
Charisma
Virgin

WRITER
Peter Gabriel

PRODUCERS
Peter Gabriel
Daniel Lanois

Peter Gabriel is an English singer-songwriter who began his career as frontman of the band Genesis from their formation in 1967 until 1975, before launching his solo career in 1977 with the first of four self-titled solo albums. His fifth, 1986's *So*, was his second UK No. 1 and his most successful release worldwide.

After seeing Otis Redding perform live at London's legendary Ram Jam Club one night in 1966, Peter Gabriel 'decided that I wanted to be a musician for life,' claiming 'it is still my favourite gig of all time.' 20 years later, for the lead single of his fifth album *So*, Gabriel recruited a brass section led by legendary trumpeter Wayne Jackson, who had backed Redding at that very gig, for his homage to the classic Stax soul sound. 'Sledgehammer' became the biggest hit for one of music's most daring innovators, becoming Gabriel's first and only No. 1 in the US. The song's animated video swept the board at the MTV Video Music Awards in 1987 with a record nine trophies, and remains the most played video in the channel's history.

TECHNICAL FOCUS

Two technical focus elements are featured in this song:

- Semiquaver pushes
- Slides

The bass part of this song features semiquaver pushes in the four bars before the verse (bars 9-12, and where this same material comes back later). You'll need to place the syncopated semiquavers accurately, taking care not to rush. Throughout the song there are lots of slides. In the chorus, these will need to be well coordinated to ensure that you land accurately and rhythmically on the first beat of each new bar.

TECHNICAL FOCUS
SLEDGEHAMMER

WORDS AND MUSIC: PETER GABRIEL

Rock ♩ = 96 (1½ bars count-in)

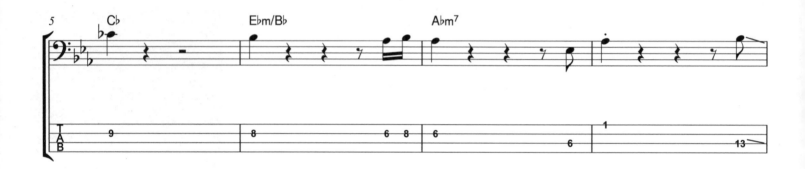

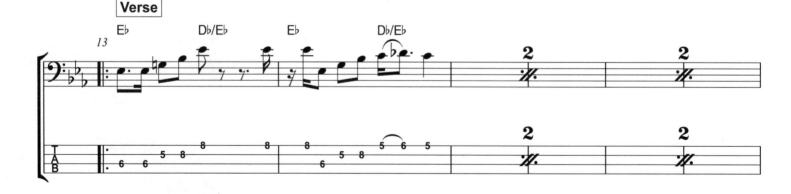

YOU KNOW I'M NO GOOD AMY WINEHOUSE

WORDS AND MUSIC: AMY WINEHOUSE

SINGLE BY
Amy Winehouse

ALBUM
Back to Black

B-SIDE
**To Know Him is to
Love Him (live)
Monkey Man
You Know I'm No Good
(Skeewiff Mix)**

RELEASED
**27 October 2006 (album)
5 January 2007 (single)**

RECORDED
**2005-2006
Chung King Studio
New York City
New York, USA
Daptone Studios
Brooklyn, New York, USA
Metropolis Studios,
London, England**

LABEL
Island

WRITER
Amy Winehouse

PRODUCER
Mark Ronson

One of the most distinctive and successful singer-songwriters of her generation, Amy Winehouse was born in London, England in 1983. She followed her 2003 debut album *Frank* with 2006's hugely successful and Grammy Award-winning *Back to Black*, a critical and commercial hit that launched her to international stardom but would prove to be her final release.

One of the highlights of Winehouse's *Back to Black*, 'You Know I'm No Good' was released as the second single from the Mark Ronson-produced album after the instant classic 'Rehab'. Both recordings featured many members of Brooklyn funk/soul band The Dap-Kings, including drummer Homer Steinweiss, keyboard player Victor Axelrod, guitarists Binky Griptite and Thomas Brenneck and bandleader/arranger Gabriel Roth. Dap-Kings members also provided the notable brass parts. The album topped the UK album chart on four occasions, becoming the UK's best-selling album of 2007 and returning to the top, one final time, for three weeks following Winehouse's tragic death in July 2011. It remains the second best-selling album of the 21st century in the UK, only Adele's *21* having outsold it.

⚡ PERFORMANCE TIPS

The bass is quite exposed at the start of this song, playing only with the drums, so make sure that you are rhythmically accurate, particularly with the semiquaver in each bar and the rest that comes before it. There are opportunities to play with poise and style throughout, including staccato markings and slides. The section just after the horn riff includes a couple of bass breaks – enjoy these while maintaining the rhythmic precision.

YOU KNOW I'M NO GOOD

WORDS AND MUSIC: AMY WINEHOUSE

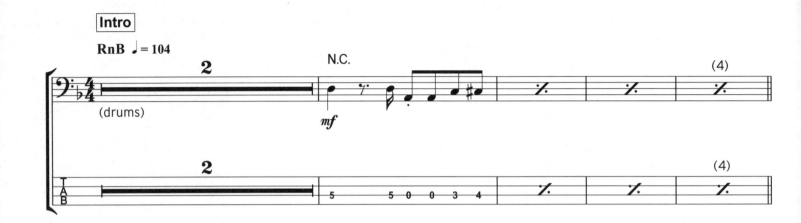

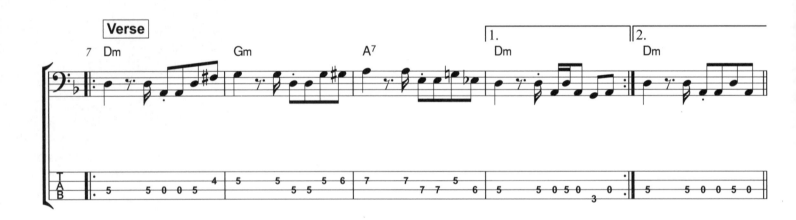

$\oplus$ **Coda**

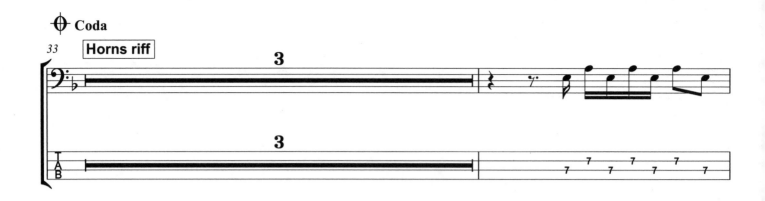

Verse

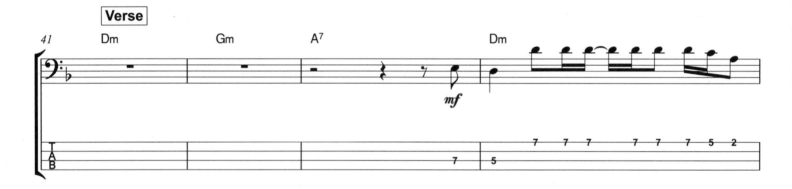

Pre-chorus

Chorus

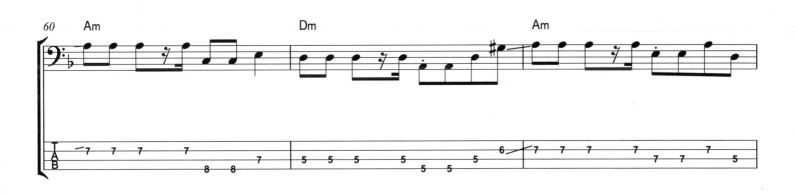

GRADE **04**
BASS

SINGLE BY
Nirvana

ALBUM
Nevermind

B-SIDE
Drain You
Even in His Youth
Aneurysm

RELEASED
10 September 1991

RECORDED
May 1991, Sound City
Studios, Van Nuys,
California, USA

LABEL
DGC Records

WRITERS
Kurt Cobain
Krist Novoselic
Dave Grohl

PRODUCER
Butch Vig

SMELLS LIKE TEEN SPIRIT
NIRVANA

WORDS AND MUSIC: KURT COBAIN, KRIST NOVOSELIC
DAVE GROHL

Please note: This song contains subject matter that some might find inappropriate for younger learners. Please refer to the Parental and Teacher Guidance at the beginning of this book for more information.

Powerhouse rock trio Nirvana exploded out of the burgeoning Seattle grunge scene of the late 80s with the release of their second album, 1991's *Nevermind*. The band were fronted by the intense figure of Kurt Cobain, whose songwriting gift and expressive voice turned the initially cult band into overnight sensations, and saw a reluctant Cobain cast as spokesman for a generation.

Released two weeks ahead of *Nevermind*, 'Smells Like Teen Spirit' was not just a global top-ten hit but a cultural phenomenon. In an interview with *Rolling Stone*, published three months before his death, Cobain said of the song:

> I was trying to write the ultimate pop song. I was basically trying to rip off the Pixies. I have to admit it... We used their sense of dynamics, being soft and quiet and then loud and hard.

The famous 'Here we are now, entertain us' line came from something Cobain 'used to say every time I used to walk into a party to break the ice.' Kathleen Hanna, the lead singer of the group Bikini Kill, gave Cobain the idea for the title when she wrote 'Kurt Smells Like Teen Spirit' on his bedroom wall. Cobain was unaware that Teen Spirit was in fact a brand of deodorant.

⚡ PERFORMANCE TIPS

In this song there should be a big difference between the mood of the intro and that of the verse, and again between the verse and the chorus. Aim to observe the written dynamics and try to respond to the differences you hear on the backing track. When you are playing the intro and the chorus, resist the urge to go completely wild – while the extreme character is important, you'll also need rhythmic precision to lock in with the guitar. Throughout, the fast slides will require dexterity.

SMELLS LIKE TEEN SPIRIT

WORDS AND MUSIC: KURT COBAIN
KRIST NOVOSELIC, DAVE GROHL

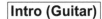

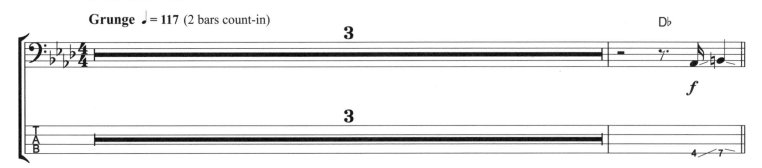

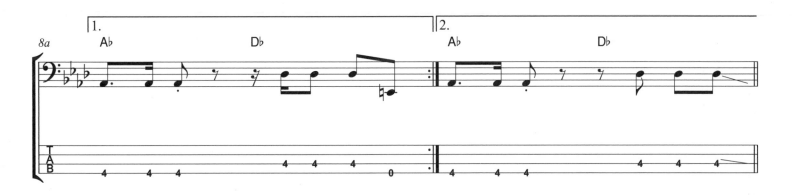

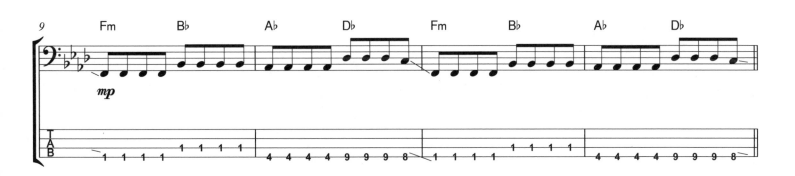

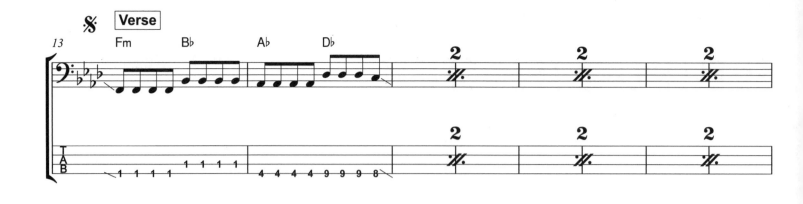

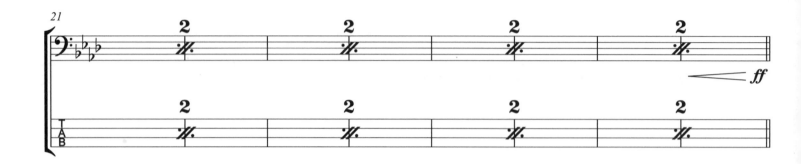

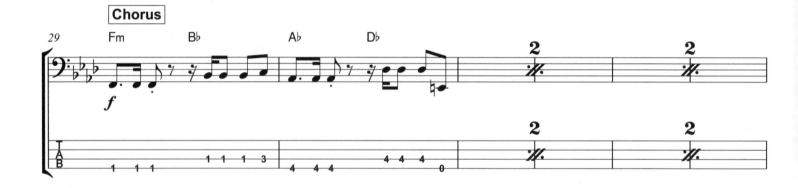

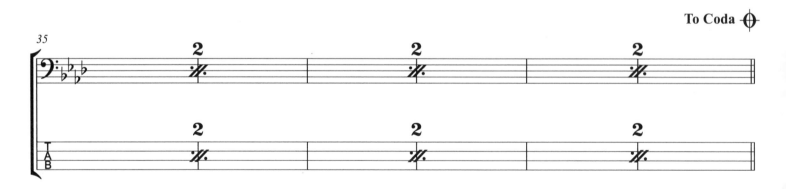

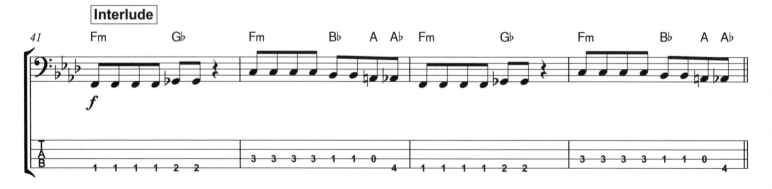

CHOOSING SONGS FOR YOUR EXAM

SONG 1

Choose a song from this book.

SONG 2

Choose a song which is:

Either a different song from this book

or from the list of additional Trinity Rock & Pop arrangements, available at trinityrock.com

or from a printed or online source

or your own arrangement

or a song that you have written yourself

You can play Song 2 unaccompanied or with a backing track (minus the bass part). If you like, you can create a backing track yourself (or with friends), add your own vocals, or be accompanied live by another musician.

The level of difficulty and length of the song should be similar to the songs in this book and match the parameters available at trinityrock.com

When choosing a song, think about:

- Does it work on my instrument?

- Are there any technical elements that are too difficult for me? (If so, perhaps save it for when you do the next grade)

- Do I enjoy playing it?

- Does it work with my other songs to create a good set list?

SONG 3: TECHNICAL FOCUS

Song 3 is designed to help you develop specific and relevant techniques in performance. Choose one of the technical focus songs from this book, which cover two specific technical elements.

SHEET MUSIC

If your choice for Song 2 is not from this book, you must provide the examiner with a photocopy. The title, writers of the song and your name should be on the sheet music. You must also bring an original copy of the book, or a download version with proof of purchase, for each song that you perform in the exam.

Your music can be:

- A lead sheet with lyrics, chords and melody line

- A chord chart with lyrics

- A full score using conventional staff notation

PLAYING WITH BACKING TRACKS

All your backing tracks can be downloaded from soundwise.co.uk

- The backing tracks begin with a click track, which sets the tempo and helps you start accurately

- Be careful to balance the volume of the backing track against your instrument

- Listen carefully to the backing track to ensure that you are playing in time

If you are creating your own backing track, here are some further tips:

- Make sure that the sound quality is of a good standard

- Think carefully about the instruments/sounds you are using on the backing track

- Avoid copying what you are playing in the exam on the backing track – it should support, not duplicate

- Do you need to include a click track at the beginning?

COPYRIGHT IN A SONG

If you are a singer, instrumentalist or songwriter it is important to know about copyright. When someone writes a song they automatically own the copyright (sometimes called 'the rights'). Copyright begins once a piece of music has been documented or recorded (eg by video, CD or score notation) and protects the interests of the creators. This means that others cannot copy it, sell it, make it available online or record it without the owner's permission or the appropriate licence.

COVER VERSIONS

- When an artist creates a new version of a song it is called a 'cover version'

- The majority of songwriters subscribe to licensing agencies, also known as 'collecting societies'. When a songwriter is a member of such an agency, the performing rights to their material are transferred to the agency (this includes cover versions of their songs)

- The agency works on the writer's behalf by issuing licences to performance venues, who report what songs have been played, which in turn means that the songwriter will receive a payment for any songs used

- You can create a cover version of a song and use it in an exam without needing a licence

There are different rules for broadcasting (eg TV, radio, internet), selling or copying (pressing CDs, DVDs etc), and for printed material, and the appropriate licences should be sought out.

YOUR
PAGE
NOTES

YOUR
PAGE
NOTES